PETER PAUPER PRESS
Fine Books and Gifts Since 1928

OUR COMPANY

In 1928, at the age of twenty-two, Peter Beilenson began printing books on a small press in the basement of his parents' home in Larchmont, New York. Peter—and later, his wife, Edna—sought to create fine books that sold at "prices even a pauper could afford."

Today, still family owned and operated, Peter Pauper Press continues to honor our founders' legacy—and our customers' expectations—of beauty, quality, and value.

Copyright © 2019
Peter Pauper Press, Inc.
202 Mamaroneck Avenue
White Plains, NY 10601 USA
All rights reserved
ISBN 978-1-4413-2996-7
Printed in China
7 6 5 4 3 2 1

Visit us at www.peterpauper.com

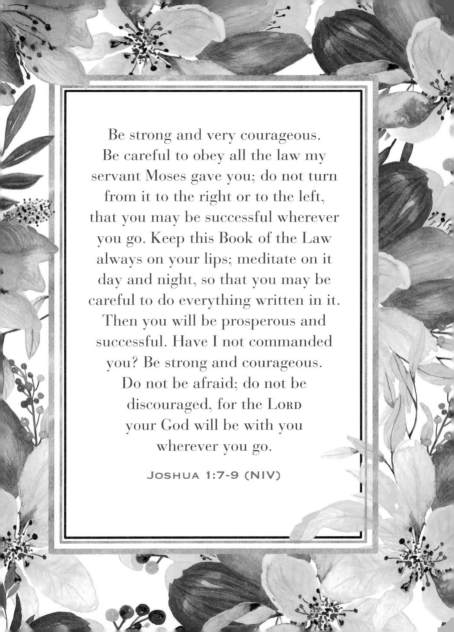

Be strong and very courageous.
Be careful to obey all the law my
servant Moses gave you; do not turn
from it to the right or to the left,
that you may be successful wherever
you go. Keep this Book of the Law
always on your lips; meditate on it
day and night, so that you may be
careful to do everything written in it.
Then you will be prosperous and
successful. Have I not commanded
you? Be strong and courageous.
Do not be afraid; do not be
discouraged, for the Lord
your God will be with you
wherever you go.

JOSHUA 1:7-9 (NIV)

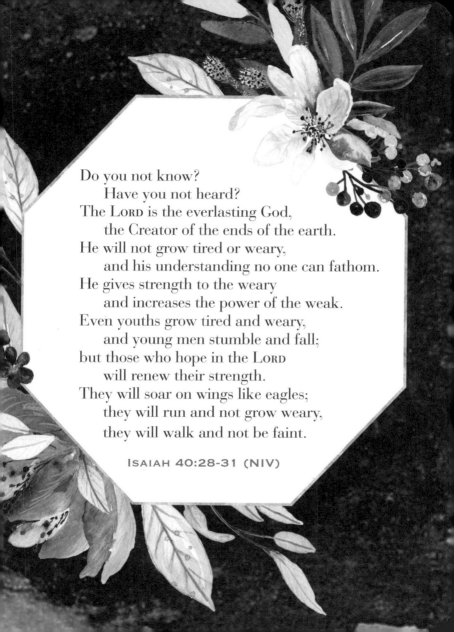

Do you not know?
Have you not heard?
The LORD is the everlasting God,
the Creator of the ends of the earth.
He will not grow tired or weary,
and his understanding no one can fathom.
He gives strength to the weary
and increases the power of the weak.
Even youths grow tired and weary,
and young men stumble and fall;
but those who hope in the LORD
will renew their strength.
They will soar on wings like eagles;
they will run and not grow weary,
they will walk and not be faint.

ISAIAH 40:28-31 (NIV)

Trust in the LORD with all your heart;
do not depend on your own understanding.
Seek his will in all you do,
and he will show you which path to take.

Joyful is the person who finds wisdom,
the one who gains understanding.
For wisdom is more profitable than silver,
and her wages are better than gold.
Wisdom is more precious than rubies;
nothing you desire can compare with her.
She offers you long life in her right hand,
and riches and honor in her left.
She will guide you down delightful paths;
all her ways are satisfying.
Wisdom is a tree of life to those who embrace her;
happy are those who hold her tightly.

PROVERBS 3:5-6, 13-18 (NLT)

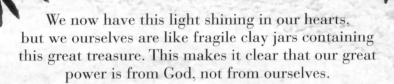

We now have this light shining in our hearts, but we ourselves are like fragile clay jars containing this great treasure. This makes it clear that our great power is from God, not from ourselves.

We are pressed on every side by troubles, but we are not crushed. We are perplexed, but not driven to despair.

That is why we never give up. Though our bodies are dying, our spirits are being renewed every day. For our present troubles are small and won't last very long. Yet they produce for us a glory that vastly outweighs them and will last forever! So we don't look at the troubles we can see now; rather, we fix our gaze on things that cannot be seen. For the things we see now will soon be gone, but the things we cannot see will last forever.

2 CORINTHIANS 4:7-8, 16-18 (NLT)

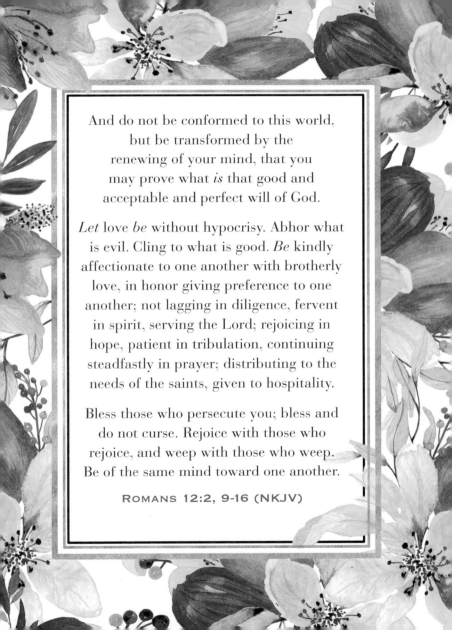

And do not be conformed to this world, but be transformed by the renewing of your mind, that you may prove what *is* that good and acceptable and perfect will of God.

Let love *be* without hypocrisy. Abhor what is evil. Cling to what is good. *Be* kindly affectionate to one another with brotherly love, in honor giving preference to one another; not lagging in diligence, fervent in spirit, serving the Lord; rejoicing in hope, patient in tribulation, continuing steadfastly in prayer; distributing to the needs of the saints, given to hospitality.

Bless those who persecute you; bless and do not curse. Rejoice with those who rejoice, and weep with those who weep. Be of the same mind toward one another.

ROMANS 12:2, 9-16 (NKJV)

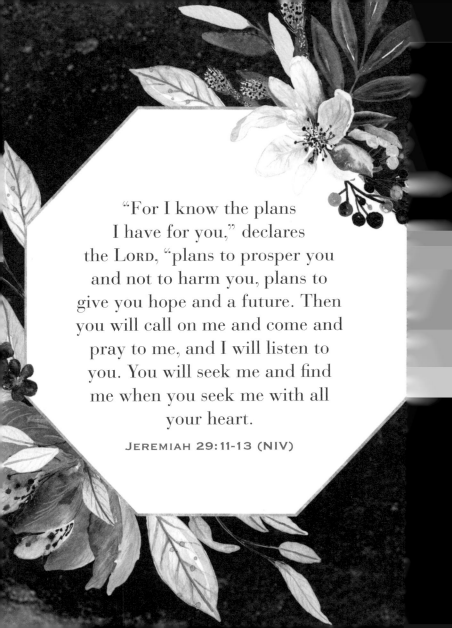

"For I know the plans
I have for you," declares
the Lord, "plans to prosper you
and not to harm you, plans to
give you hope and a future. Then
you will call on me and come and
pray to me, and I will listen to
you. You will seek me and find
me when you seek me with all
your heart.

JEREMIAH 29:11-13 (NIV)

You answer us with
awesome and righteous deeds,
God our Savior,
the hope of all the ends of the earth
and of the farthest seas,
who formed the mountains
by your power,
having armed yourself with strength,
who stilled the roaring of the seas,
the roaring of their waves,
and the turmoil of the nations.
The whole earth is filled with
awe at your wonders;
where morning dawns,
where evening fades,
you call forth songs of joy.

PSALM 65:5-8 (NIV)

So I say to you, ask,
and it will be given to
you; seek, and you will find;
knock, and it will be opened
to you. For everyone who
asks receives, and he
who seeks finds, and to him
who knocks it will be opened.

LUKE 11:9-10 (NKJV)